Google

Guide

The Beginner to Expert Guide with Tips and Tricks to Master
Google Pixel 3a/3a XL and Troubleshoot Common Problems

John White

Contents

Introduction

The Google Pixel 3a showcases Google's very best features, packaged up in a mid-range phone that offers great value for money.

With free photo storage, a camera that can see in the dark and exclusive features only found on Pixel phones, there's plenty to like.

The Google Pixel 3 and Pixel 3 XL, as well as the midrange Pixel 3a and Pixel 3a XL, are phones with hidden depths. In this guide, we've got step-by-step instructions to help you customize your new phones, dig into the best shortcuts, and uncover the most exciting features.

We'll run through some features exclusive to the Pixel line, and some that will work on any Android 9.0 Pie phone.

Getting started:

In the box

- The Google Pixel 3a comes with everything customers need to get them started on their way to enjoying their new devices.
- Google Pixel 3a with a T-Mobile nano SIM pre-inserted
- USB-C power adapter
- USB-C to USB-C cable
- Quick Start Guide
- Quick Switch Adapter
- SIM tool

Buttons and icons

There's a lot customers can do with their new devices, so here's a quick glance of some basic items:

Buttons

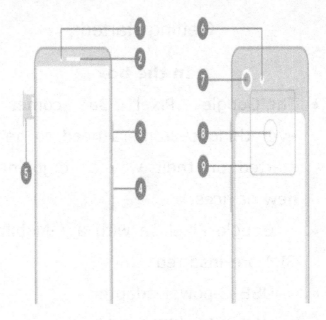

1. Front-facing camera

2. Top speaker and microphone

3. Power button

4. Volume buttons

5. SIM card tray

6. LED flash

7. Rear-facing camera

8. Fingerprint sensor (Pixel Imprint)

9. NFC

Icons

Icons

	Do not disturb: No notifications on the device
	Wi-Fi: In range / connected
	Battery saver: Battery saver is active
	Auto-rotate: Screen automatically rotates when turned
	Location services: Turn location services on or off
	Data saver: Enabled on the device
	Airplane mode: No connections. Cannot make calls, send messages, or connect to any device or Wi-Fi
	Brightness: Adjust how bright your screen is
	Bluetooth: On / connected to a device
	Cast: Share your screen with another device
	Flashlight: Use the camera flash as a flashlight
	Hotspot: Your Wi-Fi Hotspot is on and ready to share data

⊚	**Hotspot:** Your Wi-Fi Hotspot is on and ready to share data
◐	**Invert colors:** The colors on your screen are inverted
↑↓	**Mobile data:** Turn mobile data on or off
🔕	**Mute:** Device will not make any sounds
◈	**Nearby:** Find and interact with services near you
☾	**Night light:** Adjust screen color to put less strain on the eyes at night
⚙	**Settings:** Access device settings
▯	**Vibrate:** Device will vibrate, but not ring

First time use

When customers first turn on their new devices, they may see a setup wizard to help get started. Take a look at the steps below to help walk customers through the setup process if needed.

- Insert your SIM card, then press the Power button to turn your device on.
- At the welcome screen, tap Start.

- If you haven't inserted your SIM card, you'll be prompted to insert it now. Don't tap SIM-free setup, it's not supported by T-Mobile.

- Tap your Wi-Fi network to enter the password and connect. Tap Skip to move forward without connecting to Wi-Fi.

- Wait while the device checks for and installs any available updates.

- On the Copy apps & data screen, tap Next to copy data from another device.

- Tap Don't copy to skip the data copy and set up as a new device.

- Follow the on-screen prompts to begin copying your previous data to the new device.

- Sign in or create your new Gmail account. Once you have signed into your account, any backed up data will begin to download.

- Review the Google Terms of Service. If you agree to them, tap I agree.

- Review the available Google services and tap the switches to turn them on or off. Make sure to scroll to the bottom, then tap Accept.

- Review the additional legal terms, then tap I accept to accept.

- Tap Next to set up fingerprint unlocking with Pixel Imprint, then follow the steps to set up your PIN, Password, and Fingerprint. Otherwise, tap Skip.

- If you didn't set up your Pixel Imprint, you'll be prompted to set up your screen lock. Follow the on-screen step to set it up, or tap Skip.

- Tap Continue and follow the on-screen steps to set up additional services like Google Assistant, Google Pay, and your Wallpaper. Otherwise tap Leave & get reminder.

- Review any additional apps, check the ones you want to install, then tap OK.

- Make sure you install the T-Mobile apps, like Visual Voicemail and Device Unlock.

- If you don't install an app now, you can use the Play store to install it laterr.

- Review and agree to T-Mobile's Device Data Collection. When done, your device will be ready to use.

Navigation tips

While the Pixel 3 doesn't debut Android Pie - it's also on older Pixels and some other devices - it does introduce a fundamental change in navigation around Android, so we'll get you started there.

How to access Overview

Overview replaces one of the the functions of the recent apps button. A short swipe up will see the UI pop into Overview. This gives you cards for your apps which you can swipe away to the top to close, or scroll left and right through.

Quickly switch apps

Previously, a double tap on the recent apps button would switch between the last app and the current. Now that's replaced by a swipe right on the home button. For a longer scroll, you can drag to the right and hold and you'll enter a carousel to scan left or right to apps. It's basically the same as accessing Overview and scanning left or right, but it can be done with one press.

Close all open apps view overview

To shut all your apps down, you can either swipe them all away to the top in Overview, or you can scroll all the way to the end of the list and tap "clear all". That will clear out all your recent items.

How to launch Google Assistant

As before - and on most Android devices - a press and hold of the home button will launch Google Assistant. The Pixel 3 devices will also let you squeeze the handset to launch Google Assistant. You can find the options in settings > system > gestures > active edge.

How to open the apps tray

Yes, it's still a swipe up from the bottom of the display, but with Overview in the mix, you'll need a longer swipe to bypass Overview and head straight into the apps. It does work, it just takes a little getting used to.

Enable suggestions on Overview

Android Pie has "suggestions" in a couple of places. These suggestions come from your app use, so it can suggest apps you might be trying to access quickly. These have been available at the top of the apps tray for a few years, but now come to Overview - so in many cases, opening the apps tray isn't necessary. You can find the option in home settings > suggestions.

Home screen tips and tricks

The Pixel Launcher is a Pixel exclusive, giving you what Google thinks is Android's best experience. It includes some of those delicious Pixel tweaks, showcasing Android Pie's new visual design.

How to pick a live wallpaper

The Pixel offers a range of "live" wallpapers, with subtle active elements in them giving some movement to your home screen. Long press on the home screen and select wallpaper. Then head to the "living universe" section and you'll find those live wallpapers.

Engage or disable searchbox effects

Press and hold on the searchbox at the bottom of the screen and a preferences box will appear. Within this is the option to enable or disable special effects. No one knows what the special effects are, but this is where to find them.

Get calendar and travel details at top of your home screen

The At a Glance feature will let you get calendar entries and travel information from Google onto your home screen so they are easy to see. Long press on your wallpaper on the home screen and tap "home screen settings". Here you'll find the option to turn on the information you want - calendar, flights, traffic.

Have your phone automatically recognise songs

Introduced on the Pixel 2, this is a local feature on the Pixel 3 (so works offline), letting the phone listen to songs playing nearby and put the details on your lock screen. Head into settings > sounds > Now Playing to turn it on. You can also enable notifications for Now Playing.

View your Now Playing history and put a shortcut on your home screen

Identifying songs is fine, but when you get home, you'll have forgotten what it was. Don't worry, your Pixel has you covered. Head into sounds > Now Playing > Now Playing History. This lists all the songs your phone heard and the time it heard them. You can click on a song to play it - Spotify, Play Music, YouTube, etc. You can also place a shortcut on the home screen to make it easy to get to this area. It's ace.

Enable or disable home screen rotation

Head into home settings > allow home screen rotation and you can view the home screen in landscape, rather than always viewing it in portrait.

Access Discover and customize it

Android has been pushing a page to the left of the home screen for many years. It was once Google Now, now it's called Discover, a digest of topics you'll find interesting. Just swipe right to access it. In the top right-hand corner you'll find a settings menu where you can customize the content.

Turn off Discover/Google app

If you don't want this digest (above), access home setting > display Google app and you can turn it off.

Get the Pie dark theme

Head into settings > display > device theme. There are three options - light, dark and automatic. In the automatic mode, if you pick a black wallpaper the quick settings shade and apps tray also turn dark. It suits the Pixel 3 display really well.

Enable app notification dots

This was a new feature in Oreo that lets you have a dot on apps that have a notification or something to show you. It's in Android Pie too. Head into Settings > Apps & notifications > Notifications and you'll see the toggle to turn on notification dots. Or you can long press on the wallpaper and hit "home settings".

Use app shortcuts

With Android Pie certain apps have shortcuts to actions that you can access by pressing and holding their icon on the home screen. This can be taking a video or photo with a camera, navigating home with Maps, or adding contacts, plus many more. Just press and hold and it will pop up.

Create shortcut icons

Once you have your list of app shortcuts pop up on the screen as above, you can drag and place them on the screen as their own individual icons. For example, on the camera, you can drag out a shortcut to go straight to the selfie camera.

Quick Settings tips

Quick settings were good before, now they're even better. There are more options and there's far greater customisation. And remember that dark theme tip we've give you above if you want things to look really slick. In Android Pie, there's a fresh new look to things.

Swipe the fingerprint sensor to access quick settings

The top of your phone is some way away on the Pixel 3 XL, but there's a gesture to drop down the quick settings. Head into settings > system > gestures > swipe fingerprint for notifications and toggle it on. This will drop down the quick settings and/or notifications, giving easier access.

Manage quick settings icons

In Android 9 you can manage the order of the quick settings tiles by dropping down the usual shade from the top of the screen and hitting the pencil icon at the bottom to edit. Now you can re-order, add or remove new quick access toggles, making it easier to get the controls you want.

Quickly select a Wi-Fi network

Swipe down for Quick Settings, then press and hold the Wi-Fi icon. This will go directly to the Wi-Fi settings, it's great when you can't figure out what's going on with Wi-Fi.

Quickly manage Bluetooth

The same applies to Bluetooth. Swipe down the Quick Settings shade and press and hold the Bluetooth icon. If you're failing to connect to your car, you can instantly see what's going on.

Turn on torch/flashlight

There's no need for a separate app, just tap the button in Quick Settings to turn on your flash as a torch. Or just say "Ok Google, turn on torch/flashlight" and it will turn on.

Cast your screen

Want your Android device on your TV? Just swipe down and tap Cast screen and it will be sent to your Chromecast. If it's not there, add the Cast tile to your Quick Settings using the method mentioned above. Not all apps are supported though.

Display tips and tricks

Turn on always-on display: Head into Settings > Display > Advanced > Ambient display. Here you'll find the option for the always-on display, which will show the time, date, weather on your lock screen. You can turn it off to save battery life.

Turn on double tap to wake

This has been on a number of devices previously, but is now a standard Android feature. Head into Settings > Display > Advanced > Ambient display and tap on "double-tap to check phone". This only works when the always-on display (above) is turned off. Then you just double tap the screen and you'll be shown the details.

Get notifications when you lift your phone

Head into Settings > Display > Advanced >Ambient display and you can turn on the option to show you the always-on display when you lift your phone up. That means you can glance at the time and your notification icons, without having to press any buttons or anything.

Wake the display when new notifications arrive

If want the display to fully wake up when you get a new notification, this option is also in the ambient display settings (as above). You'll need to make sure you're not getting overwhelmed with notifications, or it will drain your battery a little faster.

Manage the colors of the display

This has become a big deal since the controversy surrounding the Pixel 2 XL color hue. Head into settings > display > colors and you'll find the options offered - natural, boosted or adaptive. We've found adaptive to be the best for most use cases.

Have night light automatically turn on/off at dusk and dawn

Night light aims to reduce the blue light from the display to make it better for viewing at night, reducing the brightness and the strain on your eyes. Head into Settings > Display > Night Light and you'll find all the controls. in the schedule you can customize when this happens, with automatic sunset to sunrise being an option.

Change the hue of Night Light

If you want to change the color tone of Night Light, head into the settings as above and you can change the intensity. If you find yourself regularly turning it off because it's too yellow, you could probably make it better with a hue tweak here.

Camera and photos tips

Pixel basically means camera these days and the Pixel 3 camera doesn't disappoint. It's getting a little more complicated, so here are the tips you need to get it singing sweetly.

Quick launch the camera

Double press the power/standby button to quick launch the camera, it's a great feature. The settings for this control live in Settings > System > Gestures. Here you can turn on "jump to camera" to allow quick access from any screen.

Swipe between photos, video, other camera modes

You can swipe from photo to video capture and to other modes in the camera viewfinder, which you might prefer to hit the buttons. Simply swipe up or down the screen in landscape, or left and right in portrait and you'll switch from photo to video capture.

Find the camera settings

These are no longer visible from the main camera view. As above, swipe across to "more" and tap on that option. There you'll find the settings.

Instant zoom

If you want to instantly zoom in on something and you've only got one hand free, just double tap anywhere in the viewfinder and the camera will jump to 2x zoom. This is great if you don't have a free hand to use the slider, but it's not full zoom - you can then zoom in further if you wish.

Turn off the shutter sound

That noise is pretty annoying, right? As we mentioned above, swipe across to More > Settings and you'll see the toggle for camera sounds.

Use Night Sight

One of the most impressive features of Google's Pixel Camera is a feature called Night Sight. It effectively lets you take photos at night without a flash and still produce an image that's bright, colorful and crystal-clear.

It does this using some really powerful software normally found on only the most expensive phones.

To turn on Night Sight, simply open the camera and swipe along to More. Tap on Night Sight.

Now line up your shot and press the shutter button. An important thing to note is that you'll need to hold the camera extremely still for a second or so after you've taken the picture, so while not essential, a tripod will really help.

Night Sight actually works really well during the daytime too - the key here is to experiment and see what works.

Use Smartburst and Top Shot to capture great moving action

Press and hold the shutter button and the Pixel 3 will rattle off lots of photos. Firstly, you can manually select the one with the picture you want or you can open the Google Photos to view your photos and tap the burst button bottom centre. This will have the option to only show the best photos from the burst, using Google's AI to give you the best.

Take burst photos with automatic animation

Google Photos has a great auto-animate feature which uses bursts of photos and turns them into animation. It's great for capturing not only a photo of some action, but all the activity that surrounded it. Capture the action as described above and Google Photos will automatically turn it into an animation once it recognizes a series of photos. If it doesn't do it automatically, you can force the animation to be created via the burst button in Google Photos as above.

Adjust the exposure compensation

Exposure compensation lets you lighten or darken a scene when the automatic metering doesn't quite get it right. For example, an illuminated subject on stage in a dark theatre will often automatically over-expose. Dial down the exposure and the dark part of the room will darken, returning to a more dynamic picture. Simply tap on what you want to focus on (your subject) and then on you'll see the brightness scale appear on screen. Simply drag this up or down accordingly to get the result you want.

Lock the exposure and the focus

This is a trick used by photographers to make sure that the camera locks onto the correct exposure and focus for a subject in the frame and keeps that until the photo is taken. It's useful, for example when there's a lot going on that the camera might focus on instead, perhaps things moving elsewhere in the frame. On the Pixel 3 when you tap to focus there's lock icon at the top of the exposure slider - tap this to lock.

Enable/disable Motion Photos

Like Apple's Live Photos, when you snap a photo you can have it capture a short burst of video. To enable or disable it, tap the small icon that looks like a solid circle inside a ring. You'll also find this icon in Photos app on any images that were snapped using the Motion Photo feature.

Add a manual HDR+ switch

Google Pixel 3 and Pixel 3 XL take really great photos thanks to Google's automatic HDR+ technology. If you'd rather it wasn't automatic, you can add a button to switch it on or off by heading to the camera app, open the more menu, hit settings > advanced and toggle the switch.

Get Google Lens suggestions

This is a really clever option that will highlight certain information via the camera. Just point the camera at a phone number, name or website and a link will be offered to open Chrome, place a call or open up your Contacts with that person. It's on by default, but you can find it in "more" > settings > Google Lens suggestions.

Engage Google Lens through the camera

Google Lens is an AI system that identifies objects and gives you information. You can find it in the "more" option on the camera, or you can get to it by pressing and holding in the viewfinder. Then then flips to Lens and find things for you.

Engage portrait mode

Craving that blurred background effect? Just swipe to Portrait. Then you simply have to line up your subject and take the picture. It works on both the front and back cameras.

Zoom out on the front camera for a wefie

The Pixel 3 has a wide-angle camera on the front. Simply flip to the front camera and pinch and you'll switch to the wider camera.

Engage beauty mode

Ok, it's not called beauty mode, it's called "face retouching". Hit the icon on the side with a little face and you get the option of natural and soft - or to turn it off. This can also be use in conjunction with portrait mode for the ultimate selfie. Face retouching can also be used when in portrait mode on the rear camera to make other people look better.

Engage video stabilization

Head into the settings menu and you'll find the option to turn on video stabilization.

Explore the More menu a little more

Anything that's not a main camera mode is in the more menu at the end. Here you'll find Photobooth which is fun for selfies, Photo Sphere which is a hangover from Nexus days and lets you capture 360 photos, as well as Playground which will drop AR characters into a photo. It's all a lot of fun and worth exploring.

Lock the video camera to 30fps

The Pixel camera has an auto FPS mode (when in the default 1080p) that will switch up to 60fps if it sees a reason to - for fast moving action. It can make this switch during a video, changing the frame rate. The aim is probably to give smoother results on playback via the device, but you do get the option to lock to 1080/30p - which might be useful for video makers. You'll see the icon bottom left in the viewfinder in video mode.

Apps tips and tricks

Split-screen multitasking

Android offers split-screen multitasking and it now uses Overview to control it. Swipe up to pop into Overview, then tap the app icon at the top and you'll find "split screen as an option". Tap this and it will move to the top of the screen. You can then scroll through Overview to find the second app, or open another app and it will take up the bottom of the screen.

To return to single screen/not split

If you find yourself stuck in split-screen, press the home button. If there's still an app at the top, swipe it down and it will return to full screen. Then press the home button again and you're back to normal.

Change the default app

Android lets you decide which is the default app, if you have more than one that will do the same thing. Under Settings > Apps & Notifications > Advanced you'll see the default apps option. Here you can set your default browser, launcher, SMS app and so on.

Control app permissions

Android lets you manage all the permissions for each app on an individual basis. Go to Apps & notifications, select the app and hit Permissions. This will let you toggle permissions on and off, so you can disable location access, for example.

Access Google Play Protect

This is Google's app scanning feature. If you want to find it open the Google Play app and you'll see it at the top of the "my apps & games list".

Disable picture-in-picture

Picture-in-picture will allow a thumbnail version of an app or video to play once you return to the home screen. That's great, but if you don't want it, head into apps & notifications > advanced > special app access > picture-in-picture. Here you can toggle off apps you don't want using it.

Worried about you app usage? Digital Wellbeing will help you

If you're worried about how much time you spend on your phone, then head into settings and find Digital Wellbeing. This will not only give you a breakdown of your app and phone usage, but you can set timers to help you. There's also the option to add a shortcut to your app tray so it's easy to get to.

volume tips and tricks

Notifications on Android are the best around, giving you loads of option and loads of control. But there are so many options it can get confusing.

Direct reply

With recent versions of Android you'll often be able to direct reply from any app that has it built in. Swipe down on any notification card and if there's a "reply" option, hit it and type away without leaving the screen. Sometimes the toast notifications will give you the direct reply option too, so you can reply when you're playing a game without taking your eye off the action.

Quickly switch to vibrate alerts

If you want silence, but are after vibration alerts still, then push the volume button and tap the bell on the pop-up at the side. This will switch to vibrate.

Turn down media volume

Hit the volume up or down button, and the volume slider will appear on the right-hand side. Tap the settings cog and you will access all the volume controls. Here you can turn down media volume.

Squeeze to silence alarms and calls

You can quickly silence your phone with a squeeze. Head into settings > system > gestures > active edge. At the bottom of this list you'll find the option to squeeze for silence.

Engage Do not Disturb

Swipe down Quick Settings and tap the Do Not Disturb icon. You'll be notification free.

Schedule Do not Disturb

Swipe down Quick Settings then press and hold the Do Not Disturb button. Choose Schedule > Turn on automatically and you'll find the automatic rules. Here you can set times for Do not Disturb to automatically turn on and off, like evenings or weekends.

To turn off notifications on an app

Go to Settings > Apps & notifications > Tap on the app you want. In Notifications you can block all notifications for any app on your device. Or, when you see a notification you don't want, slowly swipe it right to reveal a settings cog. Hit that and you'll be able to block notifications from that app.

Hide sensitive information in lock screen notifications

You can have lock screen notifications without too much information being revealed. Head to Settings > Security & location > Lock screen preferences. Here you can set the phone to hide information so it can't be read by everyone.

Have Now Playing recognised music appear in the notifications tray

You can opt to have recognized music appear in the notifications tray (or remove it if you don't like it). Head into settings > apps & notifications and locate Pixel ambient services. Within this app is the option to control the messages that you'll get then music is recognized.

Google Assistant tips and tricks

Google Assistant is getting into all parts of Google's devices, expanding its feature set and powers with machine learning and AI taking over the world. Here's some great things to try with Google Assistant, but hit the link below for load more tips.

Squeeze to launch Google Assistant

Head into settings > system > gestures and you can control Active Edge, set the squeeze sensitivity, or disable it if you don't like it. You can also opt to use it when the screen is off. Squeezing will start Google Assistant listening so you can just start talking.

Launch Google Assistant

If you want to launch normally, press and hold the home button. Google Assistant will pop-up and take you through to the interface where you can talk to Assistant. You will also be served results that you can tap to get more information, or to move through to over apps. If you want to type instead of talk, tap the keyboard in the right-hand corner.

Swipe up Google Assistant to see more personal information

Swipe up once you've launched Google Assistant and you'll find a load more information waiting for you. You can see what's coming up or check your commute, for example.

Turn on the Ok Google hot word

When you setup your phone, you'll be prompted to setup the Ok Google hot word. If you choose not to, you can set it up at other times easily. Just unlock your phone and say Ok Google and the setup page will open.

Open an app with Google Assistant

Simply say "Ok Google, open Netflix" and it will open Netflix or any other app. It's smart too, as for some apps, Assistant can navigation content within them - like watching a specific show on Netflix, or playing a specific artist on Spotify.

I'm feeling lucky

If you're looking for Google Assistant's Easter Egg, trying saying "I'm feeling lucky". This will take you to a trivia quiz that's loads of fun.

Pixel Stand setup tips

For the first time the third generation of Pixels has wireless charging, and its own charging stand which does more than just topping up the battery. Using some clever connectivity trickery, the stand turns your phone into a bedside assistant.

Get to Pixel Stand settings

You'd think, having the Pixel Stand, its settings would be somewhere obvious. Turns out, it isn't. Drop-down your quick settings/notification shade and long press the Bluetooth icon. This takes you to "connected devices", now tap on "previously connected devices". Here, you'll find Pixel Stand and all you need to do now is tap the settings cog next to it.

Show photo slideshow

When you first set up the Pixel Stand it'll take you through some options, asking if you want to use it as a photo frame. If you want to change the Photo Frame settings, tap on "photo frame" within the option in the Pixel Stand settings. Now you can enable or disable the feature by toggling the "Photo Frame on Ambient display" option, as well as choose a Google Photos album you want it to cycle through.

Sunrise alarm

Tapping on the Sunrise Alarm option lets you customize how the phone behaves in the 15 minutes leading up to your morning alarm, when docked on the Pixel Stand. You can toggle it on and off, as well as choose the times between which it should be active. When active, it gradually turns from red to orange to yellow in the lead up to your alarm sounding.

Screen off when dark

One setting you can enable quickly by toggling it on, is the ability for your screen to turn black when it's dark.

Do not disturb while docked

One other feature that's a quick toggle on is the setting that switches Do Not Disturb on as soon as the phone is docked in the stand.

Google Pixel 3 battery tips and tricks

Quickly access the battery details

You guessed it. Swipe down the Quick Settings area and press and hold the batter saver toggle. This will take you directly to the battery details page.

See what's eating battery

You're not instantly shown which apps are eating battery. To find these details, open the battery panel as above and tap on the menu top right. Tap battery usage and you'll get a breakdown on what's killing your battery.

Turn on battery saver

As above, in the battery area you'll find battery saver. If you want to set it up to switch on automatically when it hits 5 per cent or 15 per cent, you can do so here.

General tips and tricks

Find your Android phone using Find My Device

The easiest way is to head into your Chrome browser and type "find my device". Google will return a window that will locate your Android devices using Find My Device. You'll have to log-in to access the details, but you'll then be told the location of your phone, the battery status and what Wi-Fi network it is connected to. You'll also have the option to erase, lock or play a sound. On the device you've located, it will have a notification to say it's been found.

Get pop-up/floating navigation

You can get Google Maps to give you a floating navigation map, so you can be browsing Twitter while you follow walking directions, saving you from constantly switching apps. Just start your navigation in Google Maps and hit the home button and Maps will shrink into a floating live window you can place where you want on the screen. You can control it with the picture-in-picture controls.

Check for Android updates

You want the latest version of the software, so head into settings > system > advanced > system updates. Here you can manually check for any updates that haven't been pushed. There probably won't be anything, but at least you know how to check.

Enable developer settings

To turn on the developer settings, head into settings > system > about phone. Scroll to the bottom and repeatedly tap on the Build number. After a number of taps, you'll unlock the developer options.

Turn off the developer options

There's no magic tapping for this. Once you've unlocked those options, a new section appears in the Settings menu. Open it up and there's a toggle switch at the top. Here you can turn it off, and that menu option vanishes.

Find the Android Pie easter egg

Pie's Easter Egg is a paint app. Head into settings > system > about phone. Then tap the Android version and a card pops up. Then tap Android 9 and you'll flip to the multicolored P. Then tap the P logo a few times and you'll launch into paint. You can then scrawl, change colors and pens and have a bit of fun.

Search settings

Rather than rooting through everything, you can search the settings. Just open up the Settings menu and there's a searchbar at the top. This can basically search any setting on the phone, so it's really easy.

Find the Google Settings

There was previously an app to handle Google-specific settings, in Pie this is in the main Settings menu. This is where you'll find settings for accounts and services, backup, and transferring content to a nearby device. It's an odd collection and there's a lot of duplication, so you'll find many of these settings in individual apps too.

Storage tips and tricks

The biggest difference between Pixel and other Android devices is that those non-Google phones will give you a microSD card slot, giving you a lot more flexibility.

Automatically clear backed-up photos

There's a Smart Storage option in Oreo that will automatically clear space on your phone by removing photo and video backups. For the Pixels you have free unlimited storage for these in Google Photos, so removing that duplication from your phone presents no problem. Head into Settings > Storage > Smart Storage. Here you can set the timeframe for removal - 30, 60 or 90 days, or you can do it right away.

Free up storage space

Android Pie makes this really easy. Head into Settings > Storage and you'll see a big button saying "free up space". That will then give you a list of things you could remove, like downloads you might no longer need, or apps you never use. The latter are arranged in size and dates so you can easily tick the box and hit delete.

See which apps are using up the most storage

If storage is getting to be a problem, head into Settings > Storage and you'll get a breakdown of categories for your storage. If you find something that looks much higher than you'd expect, it's worth checking out. For example, if you've downloaded a load of videos you've watched in the "movies & TV apps" you can remove them.

How to have Google Assistant screen your calls

If a call comes in that you suspect may be spam — or you just don't want to take it — tap Screen call and Google Assistant will answer for you, saying, "Hi, the person you're calling is using a screening service from Google, and will get a copy of this conversation. Go ahead and say your name, and why you're calling."

You'll see what they say transcribed in real time on your Pixel screen and you can choose whether to answer, send a quick reply, or report as spam.

How to configure Ambient Display

We definitely recommend turning Ambient Display on, so that you can see new notifications and other information on your Pixel 3's screen even when it's locked, but you should configure it. Since battery life isn't the best, we wouldn't recommend leaving it on all the time. Go to Settings > Display > Advanced > Ambient Display and make sure that the Always on mode is off, but New notifications is on. We also turned on Double-tap to check phone and Lift to check phone, but you might feel one of those options is enough.

Never run out of space again with Smart Storage

The great advantage of choosing a Pixel phone is that everything on the device is securely backed up in the cloud using Google Drive.

Safe in the knowledge that your data is secure, Smart Storage can free up space on your phone by automatically clearing out photos and videos that are over 60 days old.

Don't panic: it's not deleting them. Instead it just removes them from the phone, leaving only the thumbnail behind. If you want to view them again, just tap on the thumbnail and your phone will instantly download the original back from the cloud.

To turn Smart Storage on, go to Settings and then tap on Storage and then turn Smart Storage on.

If you're still struggling for space remember that if you're a BT broadband customer you get free online storage through BT Cloud.

Recognise a song just by glancing at your phone

Ever heard a song playing in the background and wondered what it is?

Well rather than having to quickly scramble to open an app in time to catch it, Google's Pixel phones have a feature called Now Playing which intelligently knows what's playing and then displays it on the lock screen.

Even if you miss your chance, you can access a history of all the songs it picked up, so you can go back in time and trace the songs that were playing during a visit to a bar or on a TV show.

To turn Now Playing on go to Settings and then tap on Sound. Now tap on Now Playing and turn it on. If you want to be notified when it detects a new song just turn Notifications on.

Customize your home screen with widgets

Just like every other Android phone, the Pixel 3a's home screen is completely customizable, so you can keep it minimal or pack it full of information at a glance.

One of the ways that you can enhance your home screen is by adding Widgets - interactive elements that show you information (such as Spotify music controls, your week's calendar) without having to open that specific app.

Adding widgets is incredibly easy, simply go to the home screen and long press on any empty area. Now tap on Widgets and you'll be able to see all the widgets available.

Select the one you want by pressing and holding and then dragging it to where you want it on the home screen.

Some widgets can be resized. To change the size of a widget, press and hold on it once it has been placed and you'll see a white box with a white circle on each side. Press and hold on one of the circles and drag the box to resize it.

Capture powerful portraits with the phone's camera

The Pixel Camera isn't just good at taking nighttime images, it's also really good at capturing those portrait photos that have become the latest trend.

By using incredibly powerful software the phone can accurately detect the subject in the foreground while blurring the background, right down to individual hairs.

To take a Portrait photo, simply open the camera and swipe along until Portrait is selected. Place the subject squarely in the centre of the frame and take the picture.

Once captured, open Photos and once selected tap on the Settings icon at the bottom of the screen. The first option will let you change the filter while the second will actually let you adjust the intensity of the background blur.

Common Google Pixel 3a Problems and Fixes

Buying a brand new Smartphone always brings a very cozy feeling. A phone is actually a device with which many people are attached emotionally. Therefore, they don't compromise with their expectations and always want to own something very good for them. There are some amazing gadgets available in the markets for those who really don't mind spending a few extra bucks. Google has just unveiled its next-generation Smartphone and i.e. Pixel 3a. This Smartphone is really stunning and has everything that can help you to fill your expectations. Being a much-awaited phone, it has attracted the attention of many.

You really need not worry about anything when it comes to purchasing this phone. If you are thinking why one should invest on a phone with a high price when it has some problems associated with the same, the fact you need to keep in your mind is that these are not the major issues. In actual sense, such problems are there in almost every phone which is available in the market right now. These problems are generally caused due to compatibility reasons and therefore, it is easy to eliminate them from the phone. This post is all about how to fix the common Google Pixel 3a problems.

These problems are often confused by the users with other issues which often make them think that there is a fault in their gadget. Having a major problem in a Smartphone in its initial stage in rare. When it comes to Google, the same is almost not possible. Therefore, you can make your investment without worrying about the common Google Pixel 3a problems.

When these problems are experienced?

In most of the cases, they arrive when the users made changes to the recommended settings of the phone or don't follow any recommendation of Google. There are certain things which users have to keep in their mind while using the phone. However, they often fail in this regard and face some basic bugs. To fix them, here is the information on the common Google Pixel 3a problems which you need.

It's not necessarily always true problems usually declare their presence in the phone just because of the reasons mentioned above. There are other cases as well when the problems are reported by the users when they really don't pay any attention on the updates. In addition to this, there are other situations when the users have to face problems not mentioned in this post. This happens upon changing or altering the methods while applying them to fix a specific problem. You must make it sure that such a scenario shouldn't be followed.

Connectivity Problems

Without connecting the Smartphone with other devices in the same or different class, it is almost impossible to get the best out of them.

Thus, connectivity problems need to be troubleshooted. Here is how you can do this.

Bluetooth connectivity problems:

- Make sure the Bluetooth is not turned OFF on any of the devices which are getting connected to each other

- There are chances that the fault is there with the Bluetooth antenna of the device

- Sometimes overheating stops the Bluetooth and other connectivity features in the phone. Check the same

- Make sure the actual problem is not caused due to turning ON the safe mode on the phone

- Clear the cache data and restart the device. This can definitely work in solving the issue

- Open the primary Bluetooth settings and narrow the list of recently

connected/paired devices   with   your
phone. Restart it after doing so

- Make sure the devices have been
paired correctly to each other

- Many users have to face Bluetooth
problems just because the devices are
not within the defined Bluetooth range

- Check if the data you are exchanging
is the actual trouble creator due to a
different format or due to compatibility

- Sharing large data through Bluetooth
can sometimes cause the problem. The
data should be divided into smaller
fragments only

- In   some cases,   the   Bluetooth
problems are caused by the OS bugs in
the phone. You can fix them after
installing the new updates

- Make sure the actual fault in the
phone has not arrived just because any

hardware component is not performing its task. Check

- Swipe the data partition and check if this helps in fixing this issue

- In certain cases, the users have to face the Bluetooth issues due to hiding the phone visibility or changing the default Bluetooth settings

- Incompatibility between the versions of the Bluetooth on the devices can be a reason to this fault

- Perform a simple restart and check if this helps

Wi-Fi/Internet connectivity problems:

- Turn OFF the phone Wi-Fi and restart your phone. Check if this helps to solve the problem

- One of the major reasons for this problem is nothing but a fault with the phone Wi-Fi antenna or the antenna on your router

- Make sure to place the router at a close or a central location
- Sometimes the problem arrives only when the phone is not allowed to allow to exchange the data or when there are some restrictions on the same
- This problem can be solved with a simple reboot
- Make sure the actual fault is not caused just because your device is suffering from a hardware fault
- Check and make sure the actual fault is not caused just because your device is having something wrong with the Wi-Fi drivers
- In case the router has been installed recently, the same can have an error related to the same
- Check and make sure the problem is not derived by a virus that can be there in your phone

- Open network settings and check if the LAN settings have been changed
- Make sure the browser which you are using is having everything OK with the same
- The Wi-Fi or the internet might not be working due to the limited access on your connection
- Check if the Wi-Fi password you entered is correct
- There are chances that the network bandwidth limit has been exceeded
- Check if the cable connection on the router is improper
- This problem could be there just because the app which you are using is not operating properly
- The internet connection might be having an issue with its security. Check

Slow Performance

- Check the overall number of apps on your phone. Limit them as this can definitely make an impact on the performance

- This problem can be solved simply by rebooting the phone

- There are chances that the actual problem is caused due to a virus presence. Open the default memory and scan the same

- The installed apps when are not in a proper working state can affect largely the overall working and performance of your device

- It would be good to say not to Custom ROM as the same can be a reason you are facing this problem

- The slow operating internet connection or an issue with the phone RAM should not be confused with slow performance
- Check and make sure the games installed in the phone are not causing the slow performance
- Sometimes this problem just because you don't update the device OS
- Make sure to check the third-party apps are not responsible for this fault under any situation
- The reason to the slow performance of your Google Pixel 3a is nothing but changing the recommended settings of the device
- Do check the slow performance is not caused just because your phone is having something wrong with some of the important drivers of the same

- Prefer installing the light version for some apps and this will probably help you to boost the performance

- A hard reset can help in dealing with this fault for sure

Earpiece Sounds Robotic

- A basic restart to the phone can solve this problem. Try the same before taking any other action

- Do check and make sure the actual fault is not caused just because of a liquid damage caused to the earpiece

- If this problem arrives only when you make or receive a phone call, the signal strength might not be good or is having some noise in the same

- The signal attenuation can be a reason to this problem which can happen due to a bend on the wire

- One of the common Google Pixel 3a problems that can have a relation with the earpiece is quality. Check if the same is low

- Make sure the improper connection is not the reason to this problem. Also, check if the same is loose

- You might have selected a different sound output mode in the earpiece settings. This can give robotic sound

- Make sure the quality of music or any file which you are playing is good

- The reason you are facing this problem is nothing but a problem in the sound card or with the earpiece connector. Check the same

Screen not working properly

- This problem can arrive just because of the failure of the screen sensor. Check them properly

- One of the major reasons for this problem is nothing but a lot of oil particles on the screen which doesn't it properly

- Make sure your phone memory is not completely filled. In case it is connected with another device through any mode, disconnect the same

- The problem might be there just because your device is having its screen sharing option turned ON. Close and disconnect its screen from the third-party device and check

- Make sure the phone is not having a hardware fault or damage caused to its screen

- In some cases, this problem is the result of covering your hands with mittens or gloves

- Check and make sure the phone OS is updated to the latest version

- Check if there is a bad app in the phone which is causing this fault. At the same time, erase the data not used for a long time
- Perform a force restart and check if this helps in solving the problem
- You simply need to make sure that your device is not facing this problem just because of slow performance
- There are chances that the actual fault is present in the phone screen drivers. Check them
- If you are using a pirated accessory with your device, the same can be a reason to this problem

Poor Camera Quality

- Check and make sure this problem is not there just because the app you use to access phone camera is a third-party one and is not compatible with the device

- Do check and make sure you are not facing this problem due to not removing the transparent glass guard installed on the screen of the device when it is new

- The pictures must always be captured in the high-resolution mode without changing the actual pixel density

- Do check and make sure the problem is not caused just because your device is not charged more than 10 percent

- Most of the camera problems related with the quality of the pictures are caused due to capturing them in the burst mode

- You might be capturing the pictures from a moving object. The same can be a reason to this problem

- Simply make sure the object should be focused properly through the image stabilization option. This can help getting quality pictures

70

- The reason you are facing this problem is nothing but a fault that is associated with the hardware inside

- Sometimes the basic bugs which are associated with the OS can be held responsible for this fault

- Do check and make sure the actual problem is not there just because you use the camera zoom feature

- Clean the camera lens and check if this helps you in solving the actual problem

- The actual reason for this problem is nothing but a fault with the camera itself

Apps not working properly

- This problem could be there just because you haven't rebooted your phone after installing a new application. Check if same is the reason

- In case any application is installed in your Google Pixel 3a from any other source than Play Store, remove the same and check

- You might be facing this problem just because the phone hardware is having a trouble associated with the same

- Another reason to this problem is nothing but a virus in the phone. Check and clean the same

- One of the leading reason to this problem is nothing but changing the recommended settings of your device

- Do check and make sure the actual fault is not there just because you installed the apps in third-party storage space than in the phone default memory

- Check and make sure the app which is creating the trouble is actually compatible with the Google Pixel 3a

- You might be facing this problem just because of not giving the permissions to the apps to use your phone data

- Make sure none of the features of your device is manually disabled. It can stop many apps to operate properly

- Do check and make sure the problem is actually not associated with the phone software

- Install the latest version of all the apps on your device and check if this helps in fixing the problem

- You might be facing this problem just because the app causing the problem is having a bug in its coding

Slow Charging

- Loading your device with a lot of data can be one of the reasons for the slow charging

- The charger or the power source might be having something wrong with them. Check

- The reason you are facing this problem is nothing but running a lot of apps in the background while charging the device

- Gaming is another leading reason why some devices don't charge properly and in the defined time frame

- Check and make sure this problem is not caused just because the charging port on your Pixel 3a is having something wrong with it. Corrosion or the loose connection are the examples

- The power cable which you are using might be weak

- There are chances that the actual fault is there just because of a software issue. Installing the latest updates will probably fix this issue

- Don't make use of your phone for downloading the data or for placing the calls while charging it

- You can face this problem just because of a fault that is associated with the battery. Check the same

- Perform a basic restart and check if this helps to fix this problem

Overheating Problems

- Make sure the actual reason for this problem is not a power bank which you use often with your device to charge the same

- There are certain apps that are not designed for the Google Pixel 3a. Installing them release a lot of heat in the same and can cause this fault

- One of the major reasons for this problem is nothing but a fault associated with the charger you are using. Check it properly

- The phone ventilation system might not be functioning fully. Check and take the action required

- Scan your device against the phone virus as the same can be a reason for this problem

- Remove the last app installed by you and check if this makes a difference

- The reason you have to face this problem is nothing but a fault with the battery of your phone. Check the same

- Overheating can be caused by blocked apps in the phone or the data which is not used for a long time

- You simply need to make sure the actual reason for this problem is not related with a third-party reason such as connecting the phone with the PC through a cable

- In case a lot of apps are running, close them and reboot your device

- The reason you are facing is overcharging. Avoid the same

Poor Battery Life

- Check and make sure the actual problem is not with the battery itself. Perform a self-inspection test

- Make sure the phone and the data synchronization is not turned ON

- Simply control the screen brightness and set it to automatic mode. This will probably help in fixing this problem

- The GPS, Google maps and other features often impose some extra burden on the phone battery. Close them

- One of the reasons for this problem is nothing but installing the apps in the device which are power hungry

- The notifications should not be allowed to run in the background. Unread notifications can cause this issue

- Simply check and make sure the actual fault is not there just because your phone is having something wrong with the OS. Of course, a bug in the same can be a reason to this fault

- The bad battery life is a problem which is there just because your device power settings have been customized. Check the same

- The problem can be solved upon a simple restart. Try the same

SIM/Network Problems

- Turn OFF the device and again turn it ON. Check if this brings the network back

- Make sure the actual fault is not there just because the SIM card is manually turned OFF in the settings of your phone

- The bootloader should not be unlocked. This can invite the updates which are for a different version
- Make sure the version of the device you own is compatible with the SIM frequency
- The services you are opening or accessing on the SIM might not be active. Check and confirm the same from the network provider
- The services might be withdrawn from the SIM card. Check
- You can face this problem just because the Airplane mode is turned ON. Disable it
- The SIM card can have a physical damage on the same or if it has not been inserted correctly
- Check and make sure the actual fault is not there just because your phone is

running in the safe mode which can sometimes be a reason to this fault

- Do check if the SIM access is restricted or is locked with a password
- In case you are not using a 4G enabled SIM, the same can be a reason to this problem
- Make sure the SIM card is not having scratches or stain on the same which can block the signal
- Your SIM card needs roaming services to be activated on the same when you are travelling
- Check if your present location is not having the proper coverage for the network

We believed that all the common Google Pixel 3a problems will be gone after you carefully apply the methods listed above.